(un)EXPECTED

AN ADVENT STUDY FROM LUKE

PROPERTY OF:

Published by

Life Bible Study, LLC is a Christian Publisher serving churches and
Christian communities in order to advance the Gospel of Jesus Christ,
making disciples as we go.

Life Bible Study, LLC
5184 Caldwell Mill Road
Suite 204-221
Hoover, AL 35244

978-1-63204-071-8

1 2 3 4 5 6 / 22 21 20 19 18 17

31 Verses Every Believer Should Know™

www.lifebiblestudy.com
www.31verses.com

INTRODUCTION

One of the difficulties that seems to happen at Christmas is when someone shows up unexpectedly. If your life is like mine, there's a good chance there's no food in the fridge that can be easily offered, and the house may or may not be company ready. (We have a dog that sheds, so it's a constant battle!) And it's really a toss-up if he or she needs a bed to sleep in, because I may or may not have washed the sheets after the last guest left. My life stays so busy that I struggle with the things that are unexpected.

Jesus' birth was promised through Isaiah 700 years before it happened, and woven throughout the entire Old Testament were details of His coming. Yet, when the family arrived in Bethlehem, the town was unprepared to receive the new Messiah. For them, it was **(un)EXPECTED**.

When the star appeared in the night skies and remained over the stable, most people didn't notice it. They weren't even looking for it, even though it had also been promised. For them, it was **(un)EXPECTED**.

When the angels appeared to announce Jesus' birth to the shepherds, they were afraid. They weren't looking for anything special that evening. For them, it was **(un)EXPECTED**.

The Nativity story is full of moments that seemed **(un)EXPECTED** but shouldn't have been. This study will help you prepare for the expected—the celebration of the coming of the Messiah. As you move through this study, allow these verses to guide you as you consider how the world left the Christ-child:

> **(un)EXPECTED—not anticipated**
> **(un)HONORED—not given honor**
> **(un)SUNG—not celebrated or praised**
> **(un)SEEN—not seen or perceived.**

When the shepherds heard the angels' proclamation of the birth of the Christ-child, they rushed to the manger to see Him and then left to share the news with others. May we all come to worship the One who was promised, who was born into our world, and who willingly sacrificed His own life for ours.

And let us proclaim to the world who is still not looking for Him: *Joy to the world, the Lord has come!*

Merry Christmas.
Margie Williamson

HOW TO USE

31 Verses Every Believer Should Know: **(un)EXPECTED**

This book has been designed to lead you through a time of reflection and worship during the Advent season. **There is no right way or wrong way to use it**. But here are some ideas:

Set aside a time each day to read the devotion and reflect on the questions and suggestions. It doesn't matter if you write your responses or just think about them. If you are a visual learner, write your answers so you have a record of what God has shown you through this study. If you're not, don't write your responses. Either way, the study will work.

Each devotion has a key verse that is important. You may want to work on **memorizing** them all, or pick a couple that are especially significant to you in your faith journey and commit those to memory. It's your decision.

If you are more social and want to participate in **community**, enlist one or two others to go through the study with you. You can keep up with each other's reflections daily through email or by phone, and even meet once a week for coffee to reflect on each section of devotionals.

Remember, there are NO right ways or wrong ways to go about this. The only requirement is to open yourself the hear the voice of the Holy Spirit as you move through these devotions.

(un)EXPECTED

AN ADVENT STUDY FROM LUKE

31 verses EVERY BELIEVER SHOULD KNOW

DEVOTIONAL JOURNAL

VERSE 1

And the angel answered her, "The Holy Spirit will come upon you, and the power of the Most High will overshadow you; therefore the child to be born will be called holy—the Son of God."—Luke 1:35

With the approach of Christmas, we all have expectations for the holiday season. While these expectations may be fueled by our past experiences and family traditions, we may also feel the pressure to meet the expectations promoted by the media, our peers, and even our church. When this happens, we may be so focused on creating the "perfect" Christmas that we fail to recognize the unexpected blessings of the season.

Read Luke 1:26-38. Before the events in this passage occurred, God had not spoken to His people or their prophets for about 400 years. Living under the oppression of the Roman government, the Jewish people longed for the Messiah whom God had promised would deliver His people. Some commentators even suggest that Jewish girls dreamed of growing up to become the mother of the Messiah. While they expected the Messiah to be a descendant of King David, they apparently did not expect a young virgin to become His mother.

The angel Gabriel appeared to Mary, a young Jewish girl from Nazareth in Galilee, who was betrothed to Joseph. Because Mary had "found favor with God," Gabriel explained that she would become the mother of a son who would "be called the Son of the Most High." When Mary questioned how such a thing could happen, Gabriel said the Holy Spirit would "overshadow" her and she would conceive the Son of God. Without hesitation, Mary agreed to be "the servant of the Lord."

Even if every Jewish girl dreamed of becoming the mother of the Messiah, none of them truly expected to become pregnant while still an unmarried virgin. Instead of focusing on how her news would be accepted by her betrothed and her family, Mary praised God for this unexpected blessing in her life.

What factors have shaped your expectations for Christmas? How do those expectations affect you during the Christmas season?

How can focusing on the birth of Jesus change the way your family approaches Advent this year?

Ask God to reveal the blessings—both expected and unexpected—that He has in store for you this year. Like Mary, pause frequently to praise Him for those blessings.

VERSE 2

And she exclaimed with a loud cry, "Blessed are you among women, and blessed is the fruit of your womb!"—Luke 1:42

Have you ever wanted something so desperately that you thought about it constantly? Wished for it daily? And waited, sometimes patiently and sometimes not, to receive it? And when the weeks, months, and years went by without it, you learned to live with the disappointment, the sadness, the emptiness of not having it? And just when you'd given up all hope, your greatest wish was fulfilled? Oh, the joy! The joy was so much sweeter because you'd waited so long!

Read Luke 1:39-45. Elizabeth knew this kind of desperate wanting, this deep disappointment, and this unmatched joy. She had been married to Zechariah for many years . . . and for many years they had waited anxiously for a child . . . a wish that had never been fulfilled. Then, when Elizabeth was too old to bear children, an angel announced to Zechariah that his wife would soon give birth to the son they had always wanted (Lk. 1:8-17). Now Mary and Elizabeth were together, celebrating the upcoming births of their sons. When they met, their joy could not be contained. Elizabeth was probably the only other person who could truly understand that God could do the unexpected and impossible in Mary's life. Filled with the Holy Spirit, she blessed Mary and the Son she carried. Even Elizabeth's baby, still in his mother's womb, joined in the celebration!

Elizabeth had waited so many years for her greatest wish to be fulfilled . . . she would bear a son. The nation of Israel had waited so many years . . . centuries . . . for the birth of the Messiah. At long last, in unexpected ways, God had fulfilled His promise. The virgin would soon give birth to the promised child.

During the Christmas season, the unmet desires of our hearts can leave us feeling hopeless and sad. But focusing on the many good gifts that God has given to us can give us deep joy and contentment.

How do you deal with the disappointment resulting from unmet dreams and expectations?

How long is too long to wait for God to fulfill His promises? How does God's faithfulness to His promises bring joy to you?

What things are you most thankful for this Christmas? Pause to give Him thanks for the many blessings in your life and ask Him to help you trust Him to meet your heart's desires in His timing.

But as he considered these things, behold, an angel of the Lord appeared to him in a dream, saying, "Joseph, son of David, do not fear to take Mary as your wife, for that which is conceived in her is from the Holy Spirit."—Matthew 1:20

For many years, the fall holiday season had a certain rhythm. After Labor Day, the weather turned cooler and the days grew shorter. School children celebrated Halloween by dressing up in superhero costumes and knocking on their neighbors' doors seeking candy. The family gathered for Thanksgiving at Grandma's house, and *then* the streets and stores were decorated for Christmas and the shopping and baking began.

Read Matthew 1:18-25. Life for young Jewish men also had a certain rhythm. As they grew up, they worked with their fathers to learn the skills necessary to earn a living. They took their place in Jewish society, studied at the synagogue, and worshiped at the Temple. Their parents chose a spouse for them, and after the appropriate betrothal period, they would marry and *then* begin a family of their own. While Joseph might have expected these events to occur in his life, he certainly never expected to learn that his betrothed was pregnant long before their wedding took place. But Joseph was a kind and gracious man, so instead of stoning her as allowed by Jewish Law, he planned to quietly divorce her—until God sent an angel to tell Joseph to marry Mary and raise God's Son as his own.

Joseph listened to the angel's message and obeyed God's directive to marry Mary and became the earthly father of her son, Jesus. Through these unexpected circumstances, he experienced the joy of being part of God's plan to save His people from their sins.

Today, retailers capitalize on Christmas throughout the year as a way to boost sales and profit margins, which means that we are bombarded by Christmas decorations, music, and sales as early as July. But, when we ignore the commercialization of the season to focus on the birth of Christ, we gain the joy of knowing and celebrating the One who came to be with us.

How has your family been influenced by the way our culture celebrates Christmas?

Which aspects of those celebrations has God affirmed for your family? Are there any that God has asked you to set aside?

How could your family change the focus of your celebration of Christmas to create opportunities to share the importance of the birth of Jesus with others?

VERSE 4

I will be to him a father, and he shall be to me a son.—2 Samuel 7:14a

How do you choose a tree to bring into your home to decorate for Christmas each year? Some people visit tree farms where they walk between the rows of trees searching for the perfect one. After choosing the best tree, they hurry home to fill the branches with their favorite decorations. In her book, *The Greatest Gift*, Ann Voskamp described the importance of Jesus' family tree: "Because without the genealogy of Christ, the limbs of His past, the branches of His family, the love story of His heart . . . Its roots would be sheared. Its meaning would be stunted. The arresting pause of the miracle would be lost" (p. viii).[1]

Read 2 Samuel 7:8-14. King David, who was known as a man after God's own heart (see 1 Sam. 13:14), was Israel's greatest king. Under his rule, the twelve tribes were united into one nation. To express his gratitude to God, David planned to build a house for the Lord to replace the Tabernacle where God had dwelt among His people as they wandered through the wilderness and eventually settled in the Promised Land. But God halted David's plans. Instead, God told Nathan (His prophet) that He would grant David victory over his enemies, make his name great on the earth, and raise up an offspring from David's line who would rule over the kingdom forever. This child would be God's Son, and God would never remove His "steadfast love" from Him (v. 15).

The Jews knew that God's Son would be a descendant of David. Both Mary and Joseph could trace their ancestral roots back to King David. Yet when Jesus was born, He was not welcomed as the promised king. When He taught in the synagogue in His hometown, He was rejected because He was "the carpenter's son" (Mt. 13:55). When God fulfilled His promise in an unexpected way, the Jews refused to believe Jesus was His Son, and ultimately rejected Him and demanded His crucifixion.

---

[1] *Ann Voskamp, The Greatest Gift: Unwrapping the Full Love Story of Christmas,* Carol Stream, IL: Tyndale House Publishers, Inc. 2013.

Why do you think some people are unwilling to accept Jesus as God's Son, the One whose kingdom has been established for eternity?

What convinced you that Jesus is God's Son? Why are you confident that He will reign forever?

Which members of your family have also placed their faith in Jesus? Pause to thank God for allowing you to celebrate the birth of His Son together. Which members have yet to make this decision? Pray that God will draw them to Him this season as they celebrate Christmas with you.

VERSE 5

Therefore the Lord himself will give you a sign. Behold, the virgin shall conceive and bear a son, and shall call his name Immanuel. —Isaiah 7:14

Have you ever felt completely overwhelmed with life? When this happens at Christmas, it can be upsetting. As you drive through brightly lit neighborhoods, you feel gloomy and depressed. While others talk excitedly about their plans for the season, all you can think about is your never-ending to-do list. When your children share what's on their Christmas wish lists, you wonder how the budget will ever stretch that far. Are you left wondering when Christmas began to focus on us instead of focusing on God's gift to us?

Read Isaiah 7:10-16. When God gave Isaiah these promises, King Ahaz and the nation of Judah (the Southern Kingdom of Israel after the nation was divided after Solomon's death) felt completely overwhelmed. Judah was surrounded by nations who were conspiring together to terrify and conquer them. God sent Isaiah to assure King Ahaz that God was fully aware of their situation. Isaiah told King Ahaz to ask God for a sign that He remained in control of Judah's future. Even though Ahaz refused to do so, claiming that he would not put God to the test, God revealed the sign of His promise. Though Judah would suffer in the immediate future, God promised that a "virgin shall conceive and bear a son, and shall call his name Immanuel."

As God's chosen people, the nation of Judah probably never expected to face such overwhelming circumstances, but their unfaithfulness to God left them exposed to His judgment. Yet even in such dire conditions, God promised a Savior—a child named Immanuel—which means "God with us." But this child would be born under unexpected circumstances; He would be born to a virgin. God wanted His people to have no doubt about the identity of His Son.

From this promise, which we now know has been fulfilled in the most unexpected way, we can be assured that God is with us at all times, even when we feel overwhelmed by life.

Why do you think God promised that the Messiah would be born to a virgin? How would such an unexpected event bring glory to Him?

What aspects of life seem overwhelming to you right now? How can the assurance that God is with you help you face those things?

How could your family celebrate the expected Christmas season in unexpected ways?

VERSE 6

There shall come forth a shoot from the stump of Jesse, and a branch from his roots shall bear fruit. And the Spirit of the Lord shall rest upon him, the Spirit of wisdom and understanding, the Spirit of counsel and might, the Spirit of knowledge and the fear of the Lord.—Isaiah 11:1-2

The promise of a child is an exciting time for a family. Parents wonder who the child will favor, and as they discuss possible names for the child, they wonder who he or she will grow up to be. But if the child is born for a great purpose—such as becoming the future king of a nation—their anticipation is shared by all citizens. Though the monarchy no longer rules over England, her citizens eagerly anticipated the births of Prince Charles and Princess Diana's sons as well as Prince William and Princess Kate's children.

Read Isaiah 11:1-5. Israel's Southern Kingdom of Judah had faced many foes. The Assyrians had significantly weakened Judah when conquering the Northern Kingdom of Israel in the eighth century B.C. In invasions from 605 B.C. to 586 B.C., the Babylonians captured Judah and her capital city Jerusalem, destroyed the Temple, and took the people into exile. But God sent the prophet Isaiah to offer His people hope. Though they lived in exile, God promised a king would be born from the line of David. This king would be blessed with the Spirit of the Lord. This king would possess wisdom and understanding because he would delight in knowing and fearing God. This king would rule his people with righteousness and justice. And this king would slay the wicked.

The Babylonian exile ended and the Jews returned to their land and rebuilt Jerusalem and the Temple. Once again, they suffered under foreign oppression. Though they had eagerly anticipated the promised Messiah and King, His birth to Mary and Joseph was unexpected, and the people didn't celebrate His arrival.

As we celebrate the birth of the King this year, we can praise God for keeping His promise. We can worship the King who rules over His kingdom with justice and righteousness, offering hope to all who trust in Him.

When has the rush of daily life prevented you from celebrating the birth of the King?

Which situations in your life leave you feeling hopeless? How does the promise that Jesus faithfully offers wisdom and understanding to His people renew your hope?

How could your family share the hope found in Christ with those who seem to have no hope?

VERSE 7

He is the radiance of the glory of God and the exact imprint of his nature, and he upholds the universe by the word of his power.—Hebrews 1:3a

When you were a child, did your parents or teachers help you press your hands into wet plaster so that when the plaster hardened, your handprints would be preserved? Maybe you gave those imprints to your grandparents or parents as Christmas gifts to remind them of that special time in your life. These imprints became treasured possessions because they perfectly captured your tiny hands and served as a visual reminder of the person you have become.

Read Hebrews 1:1-6. God had spoken to the nation of Israel, His people, "at many times and in many ways" throughout their history, most notably through His prophets. The prophets foretold the birth of the Messiah, the One who would rule forever over Israel. Their predictions were fulfilled in the birth of Jesus. The writer of Hebrews emphasized that Jesus was the "exact imprint" of God's nature. The Greek word translated "imprint" has been defined as "the exact expression (the image) of any person or thing, marked likeness, precise reproduction in every respect." When Jesus appeared on earth, He perfectly and precisely revealed the glory, the power, and the character of God. And when Jesus fulfilled God the Father's plan for His life, He took His place at His Father's side in heaven where He continues to receive the praise of angels.

The Jews had many expectations of the promised Messiah, but they didn't expect Him to be the exact expression of God's glory and character, because they didn't understand that God would send His Son into the world to reveal the magnitude of His love for all people. We also live in a world that has many preconceived ideas about who Jesus is, but Scripture tells us that He revealed to us the fullness of God's glory and love.

How has your view of Jesus changed after reading these verses in Scripture?

As you reflect on Jesus' life and ministry on earth, what specific things have you learned about God?

How does celebrating the birth of Jesus each year remind you of the magnitude of God's love for you? As one who knows the blessings of God's love, how can you share that love with others this holiday season?

VERSE 8

And while they were there, the time came for her to give birth.—Luke 2:6

Every year retailers track the number of shoppers who take advantage of early sales to get their Christmas shopping done, and the number who wait until Christmas Eve to shop. Some stores have found that between 1/5 and 1/3 of all Christmas shoppers wait until the last minute. Why? Some put off shopping because they don't have the money or the time. Others are chronic procrastinators. Some consumers don't want to spend a lot of time shopping, so they wait until the last minute to grab whatever they can find.

Read Luke 2:1-7. These verses capture a moment in history: the census that Caesar Augustus, the ruler of the Roman Empire, required of all people who were subject to Rome. Mary's time to give birth came during this historical period. Also in these verses is a glimpse of eternity: the birth of God's Son whom He sent to earth to restore us back to Him. This moment was like none other that had ever occurred, or that will ever occur again.

Jesus' coming was prophesied hundreds of years before His birth, and God used Caesar Augustus' census to ensure He was born in Bethlehem. Luke described this convergence of God's plan with the events of human history: "the time came for her to give birth." There was no surprise for Mary and Joseph, because they had been told by angels of Jesus' coming. Likewise, His birth should not have been a surprise to the people of Israel. They, too, had been given the details of His birth. Yet, when He arrived, He was unhonored by those He came to serve.

The arrival of Christmas shouldn't be a surprise to us. Likewise, the birth of Christ should not have been a surprise to those who awaited His arrival, and yet they failed to honor His birth.

How do you prepare for the coming of Christmas? Do you prepare all year or do you remember it's coming around Thanksgiving? Why?

How does your preparation for Christmas honor the birth of Christ?

What could you change in your preparation of Christmas that would bring Him honor?

VERSE 9

And he shall be their peace.—Micah 5:5a

In 2015, the *New York Daily News* suggested that the shopping extravaganza called "Black Friday" would be better titled "Black-eye Friday." Their suggestion was based on the number of fights that had broken out in stores on Thanksgiving night in Kentucky, Texas, and Louisiana. In one incident, two shoppers ended up wrestling each other on the ground in the food court of the mall. In another, shoppers responded with violence when one shopper took the last pair of blue jeans available. These incidents and more were caught on video as onlookers watched in surprise.

Read Micah 5:1-5a. The prophet Micah was a contemporary of Isaiah and Amos during the 8th century B.C. As Charles Dickens wrote, "It was the best of times. It was the worst of times." Both Israel and Judah flourished economically. But, the rich became richer at the expense of the poor. The poor became poorer, overlooked, and uncared for—a direct violation of Israel's covenant agreement with God. And while the nation of Israel had become consumed with idol worship, Micah was even more concerned with the social injustices within the daily interactions of people.

Micah saw the coming judgment against Israel and he warned Israel to get ready for battle—a fight they could not win (v. 1). But for Judah, Micah saw hope—the promise of a new King who would bring peace. That peace would be the final victory for God's people against all outside powers. That peace would be celebrated throughout Israel and Judah. That peace would be experienced through a new King who would come in the form of a baby.

It's hard to accept that shopping can become a violent activity. Yet, when bargain hunters seek amazing deals that are available in very limited numbers, emotions run high, violence can erupt, and peace disappears. The essence of Christmas is the remembrance of the true peace that is found in Christ alone.

When do you experience peace at Christmas?

When or how do you experience chaos and turmoil at Christmas?

What can you do to control the chaos and turmoil so you can spend time in the peace of Christ this Christmas?

He came to his own, and his own people did not receive him.—John 1:11

One of the most poignant moments in Charles Dickens' story *A Christmas Carol* was when old Scrooge saw how little value his life had and began to make amends. In one of his final acts of restoration, Scrooge timidly appeared at the door of his nephew's home, clearly expecting to be unwelcome. Yet, his presence was greeted with surprise and then joyous welcome as he returned to the family that had loved him, even when he didn't love them.

Read John 1:10-13. In his gospel, John chose not to give the specific details of Jesus' birth. Instead, John focused on the deep theological impact of Jesus, the incarnation of God, who came to earth not just for the Jews but for the Gentiles as well. In verse 10, John used a verb translated as "know" or "recognize" that can be understood as "a flash of awareness" of who Jesus was. Jesus' own people—whose covenant agreement with God had defined their lives, to whom His coming had been promised for centuries—did not recognize Him (v. 11). There was no welcome at His arrival. There was no reception for His coming. There was no celebration for His mission. There was instead rejection.

Regardless of His lack of welcome, Jesus never turned away from His mission . . . to offer salvation and restoration to bring the people into the family of God. Although He was not welcomed, He never ceased making a way for people to be welcomed back into God's presence.

You've been welcomed into the family of God because of what Jesus came to do for you. You are a child of God because of His actions. This season, as you welcome others into your home, use that time to reflect on how God's open arms welcomed you back into His presence, regardless of what your life was like before.

Think about the moment when you believed in Jesus as your Lord and Savior. What made you certain that God was waiting for you to come back to Him?

How does your celebration of Christmas reflect your relationship with Christ?

How can you demonstrate God's welcoming arms during this season to those who do not recognize Jesus?

VERSE 11

For to us a child is born, to us a son is given; and the government shall be upon his shoulder, and his name shall be called Wonderful Counselor, Mighty God, Everlasting Father, Prince of Peace.—Isaiah 9:6

Decorating our Christmas tree every year is a walk down memory lane. Both the ornaments we have collected over the years through our travels and the collection of ornaments from our children bring to mind many memories we have shared over the years. We have handmade ornaments with our children's names on them from when they were born. And there's a collection of things they made at school and proudly hung on the tree. Those ornaments hold places of pride now. We also have newer ornaments that reflect who our children have become and that recognize their children as well. Our children have grown into adults who have purpose in their lives and who impact the lives of others daily.

Read Isaiah 9:6-7. Isaiah's prophecy was not just that a babe would be born, but that the babe would be given huge responsibilities. Imagine how Mary and Joseph must have felt as they held their newborn and realized that their baby came from God to change the world for all time. Isaiah proclaimed a series of titles as His coronation to the new King. By studying the original Hebrew titles, we gain these understandings about who Jesus came to be. As the Wonderful Counselor, the babe would have the miraculous power of design and wisdom. As the Mighty God, the babe would be the Divine Warrior with all the power needed to carry out His mission. As the Everlasting Father, the babe would have compassion for the helpless. As the Prince of Peace, the babe would fulfill the purpose of ushering in the time of lasting peace.

In the Christ-child's birth, His future was set. He came to fulfill God's mission on this earth and God's purpose for all mankind. He would grow to become the man that He was sent to be.

Have you looked at a small baby and wondered about who that babe would be one day? Did the baby grow up to meet those expectations? Why?

Put yourself with Mary and Joseph during this experience. How would you feel about this child?

How does this prophecy of who the Christ-child would become give you confidence that He is the only Son of God who came to save the world?

VERSE 12

Who, though he was in the form of God, did not count equality with God a thing to be grasped, but emptied himself, by taking the form of a servant, being born in the likeness of men.—Philippians 2:6-7

In the mid-80s, *Transformers*® were the toys that most boys requested for Christmas. The toys were unique because they looked like one thing, but could be reshaped, or transformed, into something else. Each character was a human-like robot that, by moving interlocking pieces into a different shape, could be transformed into something else, either a vehicle or a beast. And, the toys represented characters who were engaged in a great battle of good versus evil.

Read Philippians 2:5-11. Chapter 2 of Philippians is one of the great passages that explains who the Christ was and is. The small babe in Bethlehem was the Son of God, who chose to become like us. He intentionally left behind all that He is—His divine identity as the one and only Son of God, and as a member of the Trinity—to be born into this world. For God to become like us, human beings who are selfish and sinful, is a remarkable demonstration of what God was willing to do to reach us. He came in all humility—becoming like us, lowering Himself to our level—and He came in selflessness, putting aside His own identity in His mission to redeem us to God.

Jesus came to transform us into people of God, to restore us to God's presence, and to win the ultimate battle between good and evil. That's a lot of responsibility to be placed upon a small baby, but it is exactly what Jesus was born to be, and a choice He was willing to make. In His coming, we too find transformation and, with His presence in our lives, will be able to win the ultimate battle between good and evil.

What signs do you see of transformation during the Christmas season?

How have you experienced God's transformation in your life?

Read Philippians 2:6-7 two or three times, and reflect on who Jesus is and what He willingly and humbly did for you.

VERSE 13

The Spirit of the Lord is upon me, because he has anointed me to proclaim good news to the poor. He has sent me to proclaim liberty to the captives and recovering of sight to the blind, to set at liberty those who are oppressed.—Luke 4:18

Do you remember opening presents on Christmas mornings when you were a child? Probably you had already located presents under the tree with your name on them and had shaken them, at least a little bit, to try to figure out what was in them. Maybe you had trouble getting to sleep on Christmas Eve because you couldn't wait any longer to see what was in those wrapped boxes and bags. And, on Christmas morning, probably much earlier than your parents would have liked, your expectations were finally met.

Read Luke 4:16-19. Jesus was baptized by John the Baptist in the Jordan River, and then spent 40 days in the wilderness facing temptation. After the temptations, He returned home to Nazareth to the place where He had grown up as a child and spent His adult years to this point. While there, He went to the synagogue, the place where He had worshipped for most of His life, and He chose that place to announce His ministry, and those people who knew Him so well to be the first to hear of it. Jesus shared what He had come to do. He had come to liberate people . . . to release them from the bondages of sin and restore them to God. His emphasis would be on those who needed someone to intercede for them . . . the poor, the prisoners, the blind, the oppressed . . . Jesus would be the One to save them all.

Jesus' words were unexpected. The Jews had been impatiently waiting for the coming Messiah, and they had expectations about how the Messiah would lead . . . through mighty and powerful acts, through political systems, and by liberating the people of Israel from their physical bondage to Rome. They did not expect One who would be concerned with taking care of the downtrodden, the overlooked, the sick, the poor—all those who had no one to stand up for them. And they were unwilling to honor His calling.

How do you remember Christmas mornings as a child? Were your expectations met? Why?

What expectations do you have for Christmas as an adult? Are these expectations usually met? Why?

Are there ways that Jesus doesn't meet your expectations of who He should be? Why? Ask God to help you understand the role of Jesus as the Messiah who brings salvation.

VERSE 14

For the LORD comforts Zion; he comforts all her waste places and makes her wilderness like Eden, her desert like the garden of the LORD; joy and gladness will be found in her, thanksgiving and the voice of song.—Isaiah 51:3

The carol *God Rest Ye Merry Gentlemen* was written during the 15th century in a sort of rebellion against the music within the church that was written in Latin and tended to be gloomy and depressing. Outside the church, people began to write their own worship songs, and multitudes embraced the upbeat and uplifting songs. *God Rest Ye Merry Gentlemen* is an example of a hymn that accurately told the theology of the story of the birth of Christ. But the old English words do not translate easily today. In the 15th century, the word "merry" meant "mighty," the phrase is missing a comma, and the word "rest" meant "keep" or "make." It's best understood as *God keep (or make) you mighty, gentlemen.*[1]

Read Isaiah 51:1-3. As the writing in Isaiah that proclaims the coming Christ came to an end in chapters 51-52, the writer offered hope to the exiled Jews in Babylon. They had been taken in captivity, and forced into a strange and foreign land. They missed their homeland, the place where God had made a covenant relationship with them and promised them that He would be their God and they promised to be His people. These words reminded them of the mighty God who had created a mighty nation from one man, Abraham, and the words pointed them to the coming of One who would be mighty and could bring them back into God's presence.

These verses reminded the exiles that God had been in control when He told Abraham that a great nation would come from him, and that God was still in control even while they suffered in exile. And that promise still works today, as a reminder that in all situations, God is in control.

---

[1] *The Stories Behind the Best-Loved Songs of Christmas*, available at http://www.acecollins.com/Books/storiesbehindchr.html.

Read the words to *God Rest Ye Merry Gentlemen*, inserting the words "God keep ye mighty, gentlemen" into each stanza. How do these words change the way you understand the song?

How does the birth of Christ bring comfort and joy?

How has God made you "mighty"?

VERSE 15

Has not the Scripture said that the Christ comes from the offspring of David, and comes from Bethlehem, the village where David was?—John 7:42

One of the biggest disagreements to surface during the annual Christmas shopping days is whether shopkeepers and advertisers should wish shoppers "Merry Christmas" or "Happy Holidays." For some shoppers, hearing and reading "Happy Holidays" or "Seasons Greetings" negates the true purpose of the Christmas season. They feel these phrases remove the focus from Jesus for the entire season. For others, hearing and reading "Merry Christmas" is insulting to them because it points exclusively to Christianity and fails to include those who celebrate other faith traditions, such as Hanukkah and Kwanzaa. People tend to choose their side of the argument based on which statement most honors their own personal religious traditions and beliefs.

Read John 7:40-44. The people who heard Jesus' teaching earlier in chapter 7 had mixed opinions about who He was. Some saw Him as a prophet, sent by God to share His message. Others said He couldn't possibly be the Christ because He was from Galilee and not Bethlehem as had been prophesied. Still others actually recognized Him as the Christ, the One who had come from God as their Messiah, but they did nothing to honor Him. All these people heard His teaching, but they identified Him differently. They all knew of the coming of the promised Messiah, but most failed to look for Him in the person of Jesus. They all had the opportunity to recognize Jesus as the Messiah, but they honored Him not.

Today, people still see Jesus differently. Some think He was a good man in a time of history who showed us how to live. Others haven't recognized Him as the Messiah, and continue to wait on His coming. And still others recognize Him for who He is and have accepted His salvation. All people will have to make the decision of who Jesus is in their lives. And that decision will impact every moment of the rest of their lives.

How do you feel about hearing "Merry Christmas" or "Happy Holidays"?

What mixed opinions have you heard about Jesus during the Christmas season? How do those mixed opinions affect your beliefs and your understanding of Jesus?

How long did it take you to recognize the true identity of Jesus Christ? Who do you have to thank for coming to that understanding?

VERSE 16

And suddenly there was with the angel a multitude of the heavenly host praising God and saying, "Glory to God in the highest, and on earth peace among those with whom he is pleased!"—Luke 2:13-14

Make a list of all the ways your family celebrates birthdays. Maybe your list includes some of these. Even before the baby is born, family and friends throw a baby shower for the expectant mom, where she is given gifts for the baby. On the first birthday, the child gets his own cake so he can dig his hands into the frosting. During the preschool years, her birthday might be celebrated with friends at a special restaurant. During elementary years, birthdays may be celebrated at skating rinks, trampoline parks, or other activity-based venues. As children become adults, birthday celebrations may not be as elaborate, but they remain important. Why do we put so much emphasis on celebrating birthdays?

Read Luke 2:8-14. Mary and Joseph were temporarily relocated to Bethlehem to register for the census when the time came for Mary to give birth. After Jesus was born, Mary swaddled Him and laid Him in a manger. There were no baby showers. Their family and friends weren't on hand to welcome the baby home from the hospital. This Jewish son wasn't welcomed by musicians who played outside His home. The most important birth in the history of humanity wasn't celebrated with human songs, but the angels in heaven joined together in a song of epic proportion so Jesus' birth would not go unsung. Simple shepherds held front-row seats for the angel's announcement of Jesus' birth and the heavenly concert that followed. Their fear turned to worship as they witnessed these unprecedented events.

How have you felt when the most important people in your life celebrated your birthday in the ways you expected? How did their actions assure you of their love for you and the important place you hold in their lives? No matter our age, we want to know that our lives are worth celebrating.

Why is it so easy to lose sight of Christmas as the celebration of the birth of Jesus?

What steps has your family taken this year, or in years past, to celebrate the birth of our Savior?

Singing songs of praise to Jesus during the Christmas season can help to ensure that others know that He is important to us. Which songs flow freely from your lips? How can those songs reach others with the good news of Jesus' birth?

VERSE 17

The heavens declare the glory of God, and the sky above proclaims his handiwork.
—*Psalm 19:1*

Think of all the places you have been where you felt God's presence in a significant way. Did you sense His presence when you gazed into the starry sky on a crystal clear night? Were you overwhelmed with His majesty as you looked upon snow-capped mountain peaks or gazed into the depths of the Grand Canyon? Could you hear His voice when you heard the waves crash into the ocean shoreline or cascade over Niagara Falls? Maybe you felt His power in the midst of the crashing thunder and brilliant lightning of a mid-summer storm. If you've experienced God's presence in any of these situations, then you know that all of creation proclaims God's glory.

Read Psalm 19:1-6. In spite of his many failures, King David was known as a man after God's own heart, which was revealed in this song of praise to God. Simply gazing into the heavens, David saw undeniable evidence of God's glory. The rising and setting of the sun each day was the "speech" and "voice" through which God revealed Himself to David—and to all humanity. As the sun shone on every part of the earth each day, the knowledge of God was manifested both to David and to all people in every nation. Just as creation would not allow God's glory to go unsung, David would not allow his praises for God to go unsung.

For many of us, various aspects of creation play a vital part in the Christmas season. We long for colder weather and dream of a white Christmas in which snow blankets our homes in a brilliant white peace. We gaze into heaven on a clear night, counting the stars, and pondering how the God who created all things could love us so much that He sent His Son to be our Savior.

Why do you think God created a world so magnificent that every aspect of it sings of His glory?

How do the songs of creation provide undeniable evidence of God's presence and glory?

Which songs will you sing repeatedly this Christmas season? How do those songs remind you of God's glory while simultaneously revealing Him to the world?

VERSE 18

It is good to give thanks to the Lord, to sing praises to your name, O Most High.
—Psalm 92:1

Many people have said that music is the language of the heart. After all, music can express all of our feelings—from the greatest joy to the deepest sorrow—in ways that words alone often cannot convey. When you're in a great mood, what kinds of music do you hum or sing? When you're angry, what music matches your feelings? And if you're sad or depressed, how does the tempo and tone of the music change to reflect those emotions? We are so blessed that God created us with the ability to express all of our emotions to Him through the language of music and song.

Read Psalm 92:1-4. Although the author of this psalm was not identified, the purpose for the psalm was clearly given. This is the only psalm written specifically as a praise song for the Sabbath. The psalmist reminded us that it is always "good to give thanks to the Lord, to sing praises" to Him. Whether it's an ordinary day, the Sabbath (a day set aside for worship) or Christmas Day, our praises to God should never go unsung, for His steadfast love and faithfulness means that we can trust Him with all of our emotions. His works— both in this world and on our behalf—are worthy of praise, even when we don't understand everything that happens to us.

Perhaps the most beautiful music we make is when we sing praises to God, thanking Him for all He has done for us. Whether we worship with our voices or with the music created on any number of instruments, our praise is offered to God for the many great things He has done for us. During this Christmas season, may our songs of praise focus on the gift He has given us through His Son, Jesus Christ.

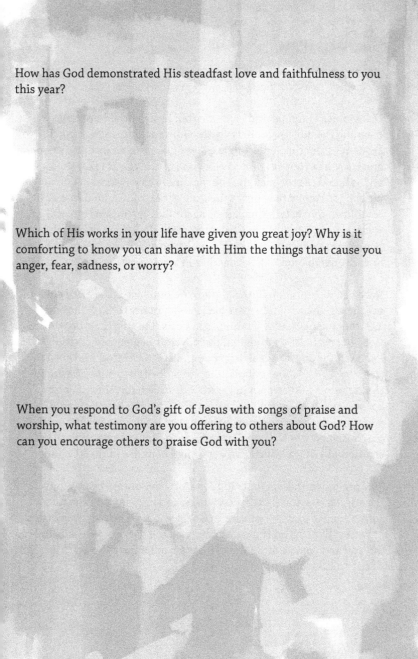

How has God demonstrated His steadfast love and faithfulness to you this year?

Which of His works in your life have given you great joy? Why is it comforting to know you can share with Him the things that cause you anger, fear, sadness, or worry?

When you respond to God's gift of Jesus with songs of praise and worship, what testimony are you offering to others about God? How can you encourage others to praise God with you?

VERSE 19

Praise the Lord! Praise the Lord from the heavens; praise him in the heights!
Praise him, all his angels; praise him, all his hosts.—Psalm 148:1-2

Many musical compositions are written in four-part harmony,
meaning the musical score is written for four voices ranging in
sequence from the highest to the lowest notes: soprano, alto, tenor,
and bass. In a chorale composition, one of the voices takes the lead
and is known as the melody. The remaining three voices create a
pleasing harmony to support the lead. When the four voices are
combined, the melody and harmony produce a stunning musical
arrangement. Most of the Christmas carols found in our church
hymnals are written in this style, which encourages every member
of the congregation to join together in singing praises to God.

Read Psalm 148:1-14. In this psalm, the psalmist called all of creation
to join together in a four-part harmony of praise to God. In verses
1-2, the psalmist called the angels in heaven to sing their praises to
God. The psalmist next invited the physical elements of creation to
join with the angels in singing their praises to the God who created
them (vv. 3-6, 9). The psalmist then described the praise offered by
the creatures God created in verses 7-8, 10. Finally, the psalmist
encouraged all the people of the earth—from the kings, princes,
and rulers to the young men, women, and children—to join together
in offering praises to God. Certainly the psalmist envisioned all of
creation offering a beautiful masterpiece of praise to their Creator.

This psalm reminds us that God's praises have always been sung—by
the angels, by nature, by the creatures, and by people. When we join
with others to sing our praises to God, we join an incredible chorus
of voices that lifts up His name before all the nations. Which songs
will you and your family sing with others in honor of God this
Christmas season?

When have you witnessed the praise of nature or creatures? What would it be like to witness the praise of angels?

Review Luke 2:8-14. What insight did Luke give us into the magnificent songs of praise offered at Jesus' birth?

Praises to God can be spontaneous as well as intentional. What times have you intentionally set aside to worship God with others? Pray that you will be sensitive to God's presence in your life each day and respond in spontaneous praise.

VERSE 20

God is spirit, and those who worship him must worship in spirit and truth.
—John 4:24

Charles Osgood, anchor of *CBS News Sunday Morning*, said: "No song captures the spirit of the season better than *White Christmas*." In the late 1930s, composer Irving Berlin, a Russian-Jewish immigrant living in Beverly Hills away from his family during the Christmas season, wrote a song expressing his desire to celebrate the holiday with family. A couple of years later, he pulled out that early rendition and rewrote the lyric. Upon completion, he told his secretary it was the best song he'd ever written. *White Christmas* aired on Bing Crosby's radio show just eighteen days after Pearl Harbor, and within a year, was a favorite among military troops. With Crosby's unmistakable voice crooning the lyrics, it has become the most popular song ever.[1]

Read John 4:19-26. In this chapter, John recorded the conversation between Jesus and the Samaritan woman. After pointing out her sin and inviting her to drink the living water He offered, she recognized Jesus as a prophet of God. She knew her forefathers worshipped God on the mountain in Samaria, and she knew the Jews worshipped God in Jerusalem. But Jesus explained that soon people would worship God "in spirit and in truth" regardless of where they were located. When the woman revealed her knowledge that the Messiah would come and reveal all things, Jesus replied that He was the One they awaited. After coming to know Jesus as her Messiah and Savior, the way she worshipped was forever changed.

Songs like *White Christmas* have helped to create an idealized vision of a lifetime of Christmas celebrations where families gather under idyllic weather conditions for happy days filled with fun activities—with no mention of celebrating the birth of the Savior who came to give us abundant life. When our focus centers on Jesus, we will celebrate Christmas in a more meaningful way.

---

[1] CBS News, "The Story of *White Christmas*." Available from https://www.cbsnews.com/news/the-story-of-white-christmas/.

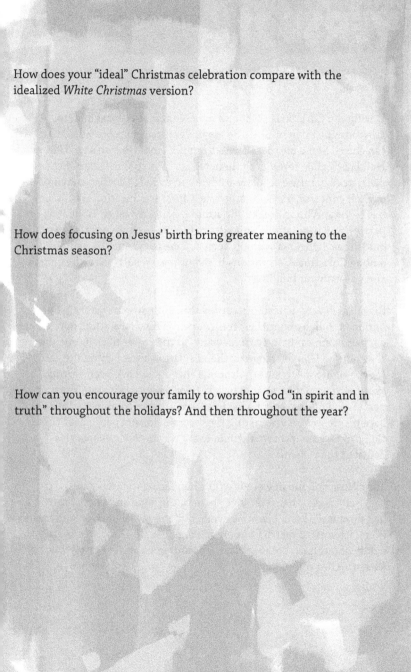

How does your "ideal" Christmas celebration compare with the idealized *White Christmas* version?

How does focusing on Jesus' birth bring greater meaning to the Christmas season?

How can you encourage your family to worship God "in spirit and in truth" throughout the holidays? And then throughout the year?

VERSE 21

You keep him in perfect peace whose mind is stayed on you, because he trusts in you.—Isaiah 26:3

During the Christmas season, it may seem that our freedom to celebrate the birth of God's Son is under attack in more ways than we can count. Some business owners require employees to say, "Happy Holidays," while forbidding them to say, "Merry Christmas." School districts may refuse to allow students to include Christmas hymns in their concerts, plays, or musicals. Christmas vacation from school has become Winter Break. Christmas parties are called Holiday parties, and decorations and gifts may have to comply with restrictive guidelines. Religious symbols such as a cross may not be allowed among Christmas decorations in public places, such as town squares and government buildings.

Read Isaiah 26:1-6. Isaiah recorded this song, which was sung by the nation of Judah about their future even as they faced the oppression of their enemies. Instead of focusing on the power of their enemies, they praised God for securing their salvation and opening the gates for the righteous to enter. Although they must have been worried about what could happen in battle, they chose to celebrate the "perfect peace" God offered them whenever they trusted completely in Him because He was an everlasting fortress, shield, and banner for them. God promised to protect them in every way possible even as He defeated their enemies.

The citizens of Judah were fearful when facing their enemies, but they sang songs that reminded them of the hope and peace that God had promised them. Likewise, when our enemies deny God and make every attempt to restrict our outspoken belief in Him, we can sing boldly of our faith because He has promised us perfect peace whenever we trust Him completely.

What attacks—small or large—threaten your peace this Christmas? How do you feel when facing those attacks?

How can you experience God's peace even as you face the threats of your enemies? The ridicule of family members, neighbors, and co-workers who do not share your faith?

On a separate sheet of paper, draw a stick figure of yourself in the center of the page. Next, draw a fortress around yourself, a large shield in your hands, and banners (flags) all around you. In the area outside the fortress, list those things that threaten you. As you contemplate this visual depiction of God's protection over you, write a prayer thanking God that He can be trusted to give you peace even when you're under attack.

Peace I leave with you; my peace I give to you. Not as the world gives do I give to you. Let not your hearts be troubled, neither let them be afraid.—John 14:27

Hark! the Herald Angels Sing was written by Charles Wesley and released in 1739 with the title "Hymn for Christmas Day." Though Wesley's original version included ten short stanzas, after changes made by several people over a number of years, the opening stanza of the song we sing today is very close to Wesley's version, and continues to reflect the message of Luke 2:14:

> *Hark! the herald angels sing,*
> *"Glory to the new-born King;*
> *Peace on earth and mercy mild,*
> *God and sinners reconciled!"*

About one hundred years later, Felix Mendelssohn composed a cantata featuring Wesley's hymn. The final four stanzas were omitted, two original short stanzas were combined into one longer stanza, and a refrain (or chorus) was added so the words fit Mendelssohn's longer upbeat melody. This final version has become the favorite Christmas song we sing today.[1]

Read John 14:25-27. On the night of Christ's birth, the angels sang: "Glory to God in the highest, and on earth peace among those with whom he is pleased!" (Lk. 2:14) Wesley's song interpreted this message as "Peace on earth and mercy mild, God and sinners reconciled!" In one of His final discussions with His disciples, Jesus assured them that He was not leaving them alone, but would send the Holy Spirit to be with them after He left. The promise Jesus made to the disciples is one He makes to us as well: "Peace I leave with you; my peace I give to you."

Because we have been reconciled to God through faith in Jesus, we can experience peace in a world filled with chaos, worry, conflict, and war. When we turn to Him, we can find the peace He promised us, and we can join with the angels in singing, "Peace on earth."

---

[1] C. Michael Hawn, "History of Hymns: "Hark! the Herald Angels Sing," available from The United Methodist Church Discipleship Ministries at https://www.umcdiscipleship.org/resources/history-of-hymns-hark-the-herald-angels-sing.

What worries or troubles lay heavily on your heart this season?

What does Jesus' promise to give you peace in the midst of your troubles mean to you?

Which people in your life are experiencing troubles, worries, and conflicts in their lives? Pray that God will give you an opportunity to share with them the peace that Jesus offers.

VERSE 23

And I heard every creature in heaven and on earth and under the earth and in the sea, and all that is in them, saying, "To him who sits on the throne and to the Lamb be blessing and honor and glory and might forever and ever!"
—Revelation 5:13

Christmas concerts are an integral part of the holiday season. Many churches spend months preparing a Christmas cantata to proclaim the gospel through music and drama. Many bands and artists also develop special Christmas concerts for their dedicated fans. In 2014, Mariah Carey announced a special slate of "All I Want For Christmas is You" concerts at her preferred venue, Beacon Theatre in New York City. Carey explained, "I can't imagine being anywhere more special than live on stage, in my hometown, celebrating with my fans during the Christmas season, my most treasured time of the year," so she scheduled "four unprecedented performances" in the week before Christmas.[1]

Read Revelation 5:11-14. While he was exiled on the island of Patmos, the apostle John was visited by an angel sent from God who revealed to John the things that would "soon take place." John's lengthy vision, recorded in the book of Revelation, included this vision of God on the throne, the living creatures, the elders, and "myriads of myriads and thousands of thousands" praising the Lamb who was slain. As we read John's words, we capture just a glimpse of the magnificence of heaven where we will, for all eternity, sing praise to God and to His Son, who offered Himself as the sacrifice for our sins.

Carey's concert featured music from her best-selling album, "Merry Christmas," which includes both secular Christmas songs and hymns celebrating the birth of Jesus. As wonderful as this live concert must have been, however, it provided no comparison to the concert of praise we will witness in heaven when "myriads of myriads" worship God the Father and the Lamb who was slain.

[1] Mariah Carey, "Mariah Announces All I Want For Christmas Is You Concerts in NYC," available from http://www.mariahcarey.com/news/title/mariah-announces-all-i-want-for-christmas-is-you-concerts-in-nyc/.

What special gatherings are most important to your celebration of Christmas? Who will be there and what will you do?

How does our celebration of Christmas on earth prepare us for the eternal celebration of God and Jesus in heaven?

As you join with others to praise God and Jesus this season, ask God for a glimpse of what an eternity in heaven spent praising God with "myriads of myriads" might be like.

VERSE 24

And when they saw it, they made known the saying that had been told them concerning this child.—Luke 2:17

The Christmas carol *Go, Tell It on the Mountain* began as a Negro spiritual sometime in the 1800s, and was passed orally from slave to slave and plantation to plantation. Toward the end of the century, John Wesley Work, Jr., son of a church choir director and a Latin and Greek scholar, with an intense love of music, become the first collector of African-American Negro spirituals, carefully creating a written record of the lyrics and the melody of many. Work published two volumes of spirituals, including *Go, Tell It on the Mountain*. His work documents not only the song itself, but also the long history of telling the story of the birth of Jesus through the song.[1]

Read Luke 2:15-20. Imagine standing in the middle of a field which has been covered in heavenly light while listening to angels sing. That experience for the shepherds was unique to that moment in time, and was something they would never forget or experience again. It changed them. And, it propelled them to find the child the angels had proclaimed and to worship Him as the angels had. Astounded by all they had seen and heard, they didn't keep that experience to themselves. They left the manger and went to tell everyone they could find what they had heard, what they had seen, and what they had experienced.

All who come to the manger have a responsibility to *Go, Tell It on the Mountain*. And the telling should never lose the uniqueness of the moment or the divineness within it.

---

[1] *Go, Tell It on the Mountain—The Story Behind the Song*; available at http://gaither.com/news/"go-tell-it-mountain"-story-behind-song.

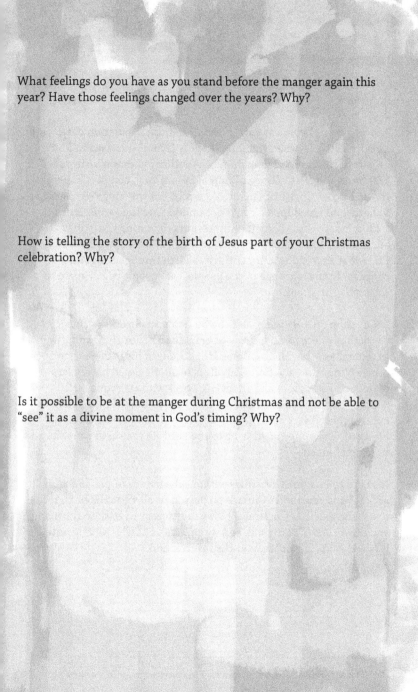

What feelings do you have as you stand before the manger again this year? Have those feelings changed over the years? Why?

How is telling the story of the birth of Jesus part of your Christmas celebration? Why?

Is it possible to be at the manger during Christmas and not be able to "see" it as a divine moment in God's timing? Why?

VERSE 25

For great is the Lord, and greatly to be praised; he is to be feared above all gods.
—*Psalm 96:4*

The singing of hymns as part of the Christmas celebration dates back as early 129 A.D. when the song "Angel's Hymn" was used in Rome as part of the church remembrance. Another hymn was written in 760 for the Greek Orthodox Church. Before long, composers began to write other Christmas hymns or carols, but the songs were written in Latin and worshippers could not understand the words. By the 1200s, most people had little interest in celebrating Christmas at all. It wasn't until 1223, when St. Francis of Assisi started Nativity Plays that shared the story of Christ's birth through songs and choruses in the language of the people, that people began again to celebrate Christmas.[1]

Read Psalm 96:1-4. The psalmist who wrote Psalm 96 saw music as a way to connect to God, a way to praise and honor Him, and a way to remember what He had done. He challenged his readers to tell others about the salvation God offers to all. He urged his readers to declare God's glory and share His works with everyone—all peoples—so that all could know Him. He encouraged his readers to express their reverence and awe of God by praising His name. And his words encourage us to "sing to the Lord" in praise, in worship, and in remembrance.

It's hard to imagine Christmas without the hymns of praise that help us "see" and remember Christ's birth, and recall what His birth means to us. The music of Christmas powerfully brings us back to the manger and before the Christ-child, and it reminds us of why we celebrate His birth, His life, His death, and His resurrection.

---

[1] *The History of Christmas Carols*; available at https://www.whychristmas.com/customs/carols_history.shtml.

How does the music of Christmas define your celebration?

What has the music of Christmas taught you about the Christ-child and His Father?

Find time to spend in worship through music this season. Reflect on the gift of the Christ-child in your life. What music speaks most clearly to you in this season?

VERSE 26

For even the Son of Man came not to be served but to serve, and to give his life as a ransom for many.—Mark 10:45

The legend of St. Nick or Santa Claus can be traced back to the work of Bishop Nicholas of Myra in the 4th century. Nicholas was brought up by devout Christian parents from whom he learned discipline and charity. He was only 15 years old when his parents died and he received a large inheritance, which he spent entirely on meeting the needs of the poor and infirm. One documented story described a man with three daughters who had lost all his money. Without dowries, the daughters could not be married and the man was going to be forced to sell them into slavery. Nicholas heard of the family's plight, and on three different occasions, he anonymously threw a bag of gold coins through an open window into the house. The bags landed on stockings or shoes set by the fireplace to dry. On the third occasion, the father saw what happened and thanked the bishop personally. This story led to some of our Christian traditions, such as the giving of presents and the hanging of stockings or putting out shoes on Christmas Eve. Nicholas was made a saint within a hundred years of his death, and many in Europe continue to celebrate his life on December 6th each year.[1]

Read Mark 10:42-45. Mark recorded Jesus' words about how His followers should live in the world. Jesus instructed them to be servants to others, to put others first, and to give themselves to others. Why? Because Jesus would do the same for them. Jesus humbled Himself when He came to us as a small baby, and He spent His life on earth showing us how to live. And then, He showed His disciples what these words meant by giving His life for us on the cross.

St. Nicholas spent his life trying to live up to Jesus' instructions by giving everything he had to others. His actions have been memorialized in many of the ways we continue to celebrate Christmas today.

---

[1] St. Nicholas Center; available at https://www.stnicholascenter.org/pages/who-is-st-nicholas/.

What does it mean to be a servant to others in today's "it's all about me" culture?

What guides your gift giving? How do you determine what you buy, what you give, and to whom you give?

What act of service has most defined your understanding of Christmas?

(UN)SEEN

VERSE 27

Again Jesus spoke to them, saying, "I am the light of the world. Whoever follows me will not walk in darkness, but will have the light of life."—John 8:12

Some of my favorite memories of Christmas as a child are of the nights we drove through neighborhoods looking at Christmas lights and singing Christmas songs and carols. The outside lights always seemed magical to me. Today, Christmas light shows and displays have grown beyond anything that could have been imagined in the 1950s and 1960s. But the tradition of Christmas lights started much earlier and on a much smaller basis. In the 17th century, people in Germany and Eastern Europe would put candles on trees which could only be burned for a few minutes for a couple of nights before Christmas. Others would burn candles in the windows of their homes. Those candles said to all who passed by that those were Christian homes celebrating Christmas and that other Christians were welcome to come join them.[1]

Read John 8:12. Throughout his gospel, John used the visual image of "light" to describe Jesus as the One who had come to dispel the darkness or the evil of the world. John's imagery was not of his own creation, however, because Jesus referred to Himself as "the light of the world." Jesus' self-identification reminded His listeners of Isaiah's prophecy which proclaimed, "the people who walked in darkness have seen a great light" (Isa. 9:2).

Christmas lights have the ability to draw people's attention and to add a sense of magic to Christmas. They also have the ability to remind us of The Light whose birth we celebrate each Christmas. In that sense, decorating our homes with lights can be a part of proclaiming to the world that the darkness cannot exist there because Jesus Christ is Lord.

---

[1] *History behind Christmas Lights*; available at http://www.highcountrylights.com/fun-activities/christmas-light-history.html.

What are your favorite memories of Christmas lights from your childhood?

What part does decorating with Christmas lights play in your current Christmas celebrations?

Light a candle and as you watch the flame flicker, reflect on the light that Jesus has brought into your life. How can that understanding become a part of your Christmas traditions?

VERSE 28

For "everyone who calls on the name of the Lord will be saved."—Romans 10:13

Charles Dickens' classic story of *The Christmas Carol* has become a holiday tradition for many. The story traced the experiences of Ebenezer Scrooge, a miserly, embittered old man who had become so focused on his own bleak effort to make money that he had lost any sense of the needs of humanity. After being visited by the Ghosts of Christmas Past, Present, and Future, Scrooge realized that his life had been wasted in selfishness, and he vowed to make up for his mistreatment of others by showing care and concern to those around him. At the end of the story, after Scrooge began making amends, little Tiny Tim, a crippled boy whose future was secured through Scrooge's changing attitude toward others, announced the story's benediction and blessing: "God bless us, everyone!"

Read Romans 10:11-13. In his treatise to the Romans, Paul emphasized this blessing from God that is available to all. He listed no distinctions of who might or might not be acceptable to receive God's blessing of salvation because there are none—not by color, race, ethnicity, past experiences, upbringing, economic status, background, biblical knowledge. The list could go on and on with every conceivable difference found in mankind. Paul stated that the only thing that determines who receives this blessing is based on the decision every person makes—whether he or she is willing to call upon the name of Jesus Christ as Savior and Lord.

Tiny Tim had it right. Christmas is the time when we can celebrate that God sent His Son in the form of a baby so that we might be saved. It is the ultimate Christmas blessing! And it is meant to be shared by the world.

Read John 3:16. How does this verse reflect the Christmas blessing of the birth of Jesus?

What does it mean to you to have chosen to accept the Christmas blessing of Jesus?

How do you share that Christmas blessing with others? If you don't intentionally share that blessing with others, prayerfully consider how God can use you to bless others during this season.

VERSE 29

For I am sure that neither death nor life, nor angels nor rulers, nor things present nor things to come, nor powers, nor height nor depth, nor anything else in all creation, will be able to separate us from the love of God in Christ Jesus our Lord.—Romans 8:38-39

Some of the most enduring Christmas movies record moments of seeing miracles happen. In *It's a Wonderful Life*, George Bailey has given up all hope until an angel shows him the value of his life and a town showers him with monies to bail him out of a terrible situation. In *Miracle on 34th Street*, the life of one man who claims to be Santa Claus miraculously impacts all those around him. Even the musical *White Christmas* ended with snow coming miraculously at just the right moment to save the inn's future. And each year, new movies are released that record a miraculous event . . . a missing loved one is found, a broken relationship restored, a struggling business is saved, or true love is discovered. Why do we have this fascination with Christmas miracles? Is it because we are all hoping for a miracle ourselves?

Read Romans 8:38-39. Paul's words are some of the most beautiful ever written about the love of God. His love endures forever and is not changed by death. His love endures beyond anything anyone, even rulers, can do. His love endures within and throughout all creation. His love endures because it cannot be removed from us, and we cannot be separated from it.

In reality, Christmas is the miracle that we remember each year . . . the miracle that God created us and loves us completely with a depth of love we cannot begin to imagine; the miracle that God sent His Son to us, to be with us, even while knowing the pain His Son would suffer for us; the miracle that a baby born in a stable in Bethlehem would have the power to change the world. All those miracles are present in the birth of Jesus, in our Christmas celebrations, and in our daily lives. We have only to look at the Nativity and remember, and to listen to the story and hear of God's abiding and unmatchable love.

Why do you think we are fascinated with miraculous events at Christmas?

Look up the definition of "miraculous." What moments of miraculous events always draw your attention in the Nativity story?

Read Romans 8:38-39 slowly, pausing to reflect on each phrase. How would you describe the depth of God's love in your life?

VERSE 30

Praise the Lord! I will give thanks to the Lord with my whole heart, in the company of the upright, in the congregation. —Psalm 111:1

In his classic story *How the Grinch Stole Christmas*, Dr. Seuss told the story of the Grinch who hated Christmas, hated singing, and hated people. After years and years of putting up with the noise and gaiety of the Whos down in Who-ville as they celebrated Christmas, the Grinch snapped and set out to stop Christmas from coming by stealing all the gifts, food, and even joy, from the town. What the Grinch discovered, however, was that the trappings of Christmas didn't define the season, and they weren't necessary for Christmas to be celebrated. From far away, he heard the growing sound of joy rising above the village, even from the place of empty decorations and gifts he had left behind. Dr. Seuss recorded the Grinch's redemption with the words: "'Maybe Christmas . . . perhaps . . . means a little bit more!' And what happened then . . . ? Well . . . in Who-ville they say that the Grinch's small heart grew three sizes that day!'"[1]

Read Psalm 111:1-4. The psalmist pointed out two keys to praising the Lord. First, he emphasized that the worshipper's heart was to be whole, undivided in loyalty to God. Second, he described the worship taking place "in the company of the upright, in the congregation." He visualized voices coming together as one, worshipping in unity as the sound of the voices grew louder in an offering of praise to God.

Dr. Seuss used the picture of the raised voices, singing in unity and celebration as the thing that turned the Grinch's heart. And while Dr. Seuss' book was never meant to represent a biblical story, it gives a picture of how the praises of our hearts honor God and can impact those who hear them.

---

[1] *How The Grinch Stole Christmas*, available at https://prezi.com/mwwuta0ortbz/dr-seuss-the-grinch-who-stole-christmas/; lyrics obtained at https://prezi.com/mwwuta0ortbz/dr-seuss-the-grinch-who-stole-christmas/.

Do you remember the story of the Grinch? What do you think was the person or the experience that led him to redemption?

Do you ever feel like you're becoming a Grinch in the commercialism of Christmas? How do you prevent that from happening?

How do you participate in raised voices of praise? Are you a participant or an observer?

VERSE 31

And the Word became flesh and dwelt among us, and we have seen his glory, glory as of the only Son from the Father, full of grace and truth.—John 1:14

George Frideric Handel wrote the piece we know as "The Hallelujah Chorus" as a part of a larger work entitled *The Messiah*. The entire work was written in only twenty-four days. Handel based "The Hallelujah Chorus" on three passages from the book of Revelation, each of which gives a visual image of praising God in His glory. At the time, Handel was drowning in debt and suffering from depression. At one point during his time of composing, his assistant called out to Handel but received no response. When the assistant opened the door to Handel's workroom, he saw tears flowing down Handel's face. Handel held up the pages of "The Hallelujah Chorus," and said, "I have seen the face of God." Although Handel was a prolific composer of more than 200 works, "The Hallelujah Chorus" became his greatest achievement.[1]

Read John 1:14-18. In these verses, John captured the essence of the events of the birth of Christ—the fulfillment of the promise of the coming Messiah, the divine star in the night sky, the hosts of angels singing God's praises, the worship of the humble shepherds, the visit of the Magi—all of the things that proclaimed God's glory. The coming of the Messiah in that stable that night was unseen by the masses, but celebrated by all who were allowed to view it first hand.

"The Hallelujah Chorus" from *The Messiah* allows musicians and audiences alike to worship God, to revel in His glory, and to raise their praises to Him. And in so doing, they not only celebrate the birth of His Son, but they have the opportunity to see the face of God.

---

[1] *George Frideric Handel and the Story of the Hallelujah Chorus;* available at http://playpiano.com/wordpress/composers/george-frideric-handel-and-the-story-of-the-hallelujah-chorus.

How do you see God's glory in the Christmas story?

How does your life reflect God's glory?

Go to www.youtube.com and search for "The Hallelujah Chorus." Listen to it prayerfully and reflect upon the glory of God. Thank God for the birth of His Son and what that means in your life.

CLOSING

You've spent a month in prayer and reflection on the birth of Jesus, the Christ-child. But this study shouldn't be the end. The Bible holds evidence of proclamations of Jesus' coming, of His earthly ministry, and of His death and resurrection.

Our prayer is that your study led you to approach the Christmas season with new insights and a renewed commitment, and that you continue to desire to know more about God today than you did when you began this study. We pray that you'll know more about God tomorrow than you do today, and more the day after that, and the day after that, and . . . you get the picture.

So what's next? Consider following up this study up with ***Jesus' Teaching in Jerusalem: A Lenten Study***, which will be available in February and carry you through Easter.

Or, check out Launch, our on-going curriculum, which will lead you on a venture that can deepen your relationship with God and enhance your faith journey. This study can also be done in short modules to meet personal needs.

Whatever you choose to do next, we challenge you to continue digging. Continue praying. Continue learning. Continue growing. Continue the journey . . .

The prophet Isaiah proclaimed, *"Therefore the Lord himself will give you a sign. Behold, the virgin shall conceive and bear a son, and shall call his name Immanuel."* There should be nothing unexpected in our worship of the Christ-child. May your celebration of Him become a time of renewed study of and gratitude for this One God sent to be with us.

Margie Williamson
Editor

ABOUT THE AUTHORS

Roberta Watson has been married to Todd for more than thirty years, and they have two adult children. Their family has continued some of the long-held traditions she celebrated with her family as a child: decorating their home for Christmas, participating in Christmas musicals, visiting with family and friends, driving through light shows in neighborhoods and parks, and choosing special gifts for each other. These traditions, passed through generations, encouraged them to honor the birth of Jesus in their celebrations. She enjoys contributing to Life Bible Study's curriculum and devotionals as a way to encourage others to focus attention on what matters most during the season—celebrating the birth of our Savior.

While completing a Master of Arts in Christian Education at New Orleans Baptist Theological Seminary, Roberta began writing for Student Life Bible Study in 2004. She has also served as a Sunday School teacher and Women's Ministry leader in her church while continuing to work as a writer and editor with Life Bible Study.

Margie Williamson loves Christmas . . . the smells, the decorations, the food, the music, and those she gets to reconnect with over the season. Some of her most prized possessions are the handmade ornaments her children made, and the Nativity sets from Jerusalem and Thailand. She was thrilled to participate in this book not only as an editor, but as a writer as well.

Margie has been writing devotionals and lesson materials since 1982, and has been working as an editor since 2007. She's discovered that both writing and editing lead to continued learning about God and His Word. Margie completed her undergraduate work at the University of Georgia, and her master's degree and her Ph.D. at the New Orleans Baptist Theological Seminary. Besides devotionals and lessons, she has written and published articles, poetry, textbook chapters, a training book of Youth Sunday School Workers, and a series of research articles in the Christian Education Journal. Her latest publication is a story she wrote about her mom in *Chicken Soup for the Soul: Best Mom Ever!*

ACKNOWLEDGMENTS

Publisher
John Herring

Design Editor
Margie Williamson

Editor
Roberta Watson

Graphic Design
Craig Robertson

Publishing Assistant
Bradley Isbell